Landscapes
and
Architectures

Kendall Dunkelberg

Florida Literary Foundation Press
Sarasota, Florida

ISBN: 1-891855-22-0

Library of Congress Control Number: 2001-135339

Design, typography, and cover photograph by the author.
Photograph of the author by Kim Whitehead.
Manufactured in the United States of America by McNaughton & Gunn, Inc. of Saline, Michigan.

Acknowledgments

Big Two-Hearted "In Copenhagen"
Black Fly Review "Oasis"
Brass City "In Your Sunset" and "La Luna"
Cornfield Review "Swimming"
Eratica "Song of the Carp" and "These Grackles"
Farmer's Market "The Heart's Time," "There Is No Danger,"
        and "This is not a poem"
Fresh Ground "The Direction of the Wind"
The Literary Review "Landscapes and Architectures"
        and "Persia"
Mudfish "Muskmelon"
Oyez Review "Introspection" and "Objects"
The Poet's Edge "Moon Dancer," "Love Potion #32,"
        and "In Your Apartment"
Skylark "Letter" and "Photograph"
Slipstream "A Common Occurrence"
SnowApple "The Silence of Trees"
A Summer's Reading "When I'm Old"

Middle English sections of "It's Merry While Summer Lasts"
reprinted from *Early English Lyrics*, ed. E. K. Chambers and
F. Sidgwick, London: Sidgewick & Jackson, Ltd., 1907.

Also by Kendall Dunkelberg:
Hercules, Richelieu, and Nostradamus
translations of the Belgian poet, Paul Snoek

Contents

No Danger
There Is No Danger 8
It Rained This Morning 9
The Heart's Time 10
Climbing Crook Neck Mountain 11
Swimming I-V 12
This is not a poem 17
The Grackle 18
The Silences 21
Polio 22
Reverence 23
Kelder Jazz 24
On the Back Burner 25

Oasis
Introspection 28
In Copenhagen 29
Bus Scene 30
Objects 31
Muskmelon 32
Oasis 33
Song of the Carp 34
The Fragility of Bodies 35
Mt. Parnassus Chicago 36
City Pastoral 37
The Trash Man 38
Now That You're Gone 39
These Grackles 40
Photograph 41
Some Thoughts on Chicago 42

Landscapes and Architectures
Fragment 46
It's Merry While Summer Lasts 47

Airport '88, Another Midair Collision 50
Four Songs for Data Processing 53
Breaking Bones 56
Landscapes and Architectures 58
Insomnia 61
Stars 63

In Your Sunset
The surrealism of driving 66
A Common Occurrence 67
Tie-Dye 68
In Your Apartment 69
Love Potion #32 70
Crackerjack Puzzle 71
In Your Sunset 72
The Egrets 73
Letter 74
When I'm Old 75
In a Park 76
La Luna 77

The Coldest January
Habitation 80
Dream Poem 81
Texas Canyon 82
Tucson 83
The Direction of the Wind 84
The Siren 85
Cool New Kitchen 86
Moon Dancer 87
Persia 88
The Coldest January 90
The Silence of Trees 92
On Barton Creek 93

No Danger

There Is No Danger

There is no danger
in Mid-America.
There is no danger
in these rabbit-infested
squirrel-governed cities
that sprout amidst the corn.

There is no danger
for the farmers, the
grain elevator operators,
bankers, JC's, good
Christian men all.

There is no danger here—
only rootworm, cutworm
psoriasis, and
the income tax.

There is no danger here,
no danger, just
the rustling dust
in the withered stalks.

It Rained This Morning

It rained this morning;
fire warning, none.
Violets and daisies
rose again in the ditch,
the underbrush regreened.

It rained this morning.
It stormed. It hailed.
The fever broke
under the pelting fall
of the freezing, scalding balls.

It rained this morning.
My hair is sopping wet.
My limbs hang limp
like the rain-soaked pines,
but my mind feels the weeds.

The Heart's Time

When the ice boils in the sun,
when the trees lose their leaves to the flames,
when the deer run,
the whole herd seeking rain
then you know that the heart's time has come.

When the night strikes fire in the lake,
when the air churns a viscous oily squall,
when the sky breaks,
branches crack and fall
then the heart strains, time aches.

Then lips touch tongues' tips,
eyes flash lightning in blue eyes,
fingers lay ice on the spine,
and hands burn hail up thighs.

When the steam smokes from the pines,
when the water recedes from the ground,
when the geese fly
to the south plowing clouds,
then the heart laughs, takes time.

Climbing Crook Neck Mountain

She lags behind me as it starts to rain
cold drops that drizzle down our warm wool coats.
She stops, turns. Forgetting her I claw
my cold wet way up Crook Neck Mountain's side.

Below, she sees the valley warmed in sun.
A small town glows orange, red, and gold.
She sees a shadow sliding up the hill,
a promise lingering upon the ground.

Above, she sees the dark, boiling clouds.
They drop ice rain upon her face and mine.
She waits for sun that bathes a maple tree
bright red. It seems but inches from her gaze.

A yard above the tree, the shadow stops,
clouds held in check by Crook Neck Mountain's peak.
She waits, hopes, then turning round follows
behind me on our climb into the storm.

Swimming

I

Black ants
and mosquitoes
bite my legs.
Fish nibble
their way up my thighs.
Late at night
we swim.
And after,
bare breasts,
soft flannel.

II

The lights on the shore
are just closer stars
wrapped in the black
lake of sky.

It is so still the ripples
stretch on above us
to rejoin the moon.

Trying to name the stars,
I say I see Virgo.
You say there are so many
triangles up there.

My head spins slowly.
There is nothing beneath my feet
but the fish swimming in the sky.

III

The young brave dove, ice autumn
water encasing him, stroke
for stroke to the island.

The Manitowish people
gathered a tithe of the harvest
loaded canoes and set out.

Two hundred years later
I follow their path.
It is summer, yet I gasp,
have to stop, float awhile.

Already sunning on the rocks,
you wave. I kick my legs,
stretch my arms, pull
this fragile body through the lake.

IV

I lie on my stomach in sand
and feel the mark along
each side of my gut
where hot beach stops
and cool air begins.

The sun scalds my back.
The waves boil in my ears.
My right hand holds a small shell;
my left clasps your thumb.

Your nose and one eyebrow
rise from the beach, corniced
in my Romanesque armpit arch.
A strand of hair crosses your cheek,
and I can feel the moist hiss
of your breath on my arm.

I toss. I stare at the ceiling.
I can't get to sleep here
in my basement in Illinois.

V

Four miles out, a fog horn sounds.
Another fog horn halloos.
Two ships pass slowly,
port to starboard,
red and green.

On the beach
we search for their silhouettes
but see nothing except the sky
waving wildly before our eyes.

It is cold and our elbows
quiver beneath the binoculars.

I try to find the moon
but it slips past one lens,
eludes the other altogether,

as a ranger's searchlight
sweeps us from the shore
back through the paths
in the dunes to where

the only ships are stars
that bellow the night alive.

This is not a poem...

This is not a poem
  this is a bird in your rear view mirror.
This is a thought rising
  from a field of harvested corn
  heavy from the weight of kernels
  missed by the combine.
It finds a current of warm air
  above the highway. Lifts
  to a safe altitude, finally.

Perhaps you are on your way to your lover.
Or maybe you're just out driving.
This makes you pull over,
this half-formed thought, black
wings in the periphery of your vision.

This is a blackbird.
This is a cornfield.
This is a fine day
  for a drive.

The Grackle

I will become a grackle, one of those
dirty birds you abhor, with dust and fleas
in my wings and lice in the feathers on my chest.
And I will fly to you, crossing a hundred miles of fields.
I will fly into your window in the night,
a hundred times against the glass, till you wake
to see me lying stunned in the grass.

I will strut through the dew in the morning,
pacing patterns around your yard,
and I'll taunt you till you go for your gun,
but I will not fly away. I know
the Winchester's unloaded.
So I will wait till you step outside,
then rise and fly in your face
and tailspin back to the ground
to grovel for mercy at your feet.

You will prod me with your crutch tip,
and I will play dead as you roll me over
and stare at you blankly with my small glassy eyes.
You will go for your dandelion digger, your stick
with the sharp forked tongue. But when you return
to finish me off, I will no longer be there.

I'll be in our maple tree,
hiding like a child in the leaves.
I'll see you shake your head
and walk stiffly indoors.
Then I'll fly down the chimney
to make you hear me flap
in the bowels of the house,
as if I were trying to get in.

But the flue's always closed,
so I'll flap just to frighten you.
I'll flap up and down till you take
your stick and bang on the hearth.

And I will keep flapping,
and you will keep banging,
till the noise is so great
we both have to sit.

You'll settle in your chair
and I in the iron soot of the flue.
Then you will know who I am.
I will listen for you to call out
my name, and I will caw,
so the grackle in you will know.

~ ~ ~ ~ ~ ~

Now I must put on these wings.
They are tight these crutches of a bird.
And my feet are cramped in these iron claws.
My feathers itch and I curse the god who made lice
but it's a small price to pay for flight.

I can learn to catch flies with my beak.
I can learn to move with my wings and let my legs
swing limp, paralyzed like yours.
I can learn to steer with my tail
and to follow my backwards binocular eyes.

I have come to see you, father.
Do you see me here with a murder of crows in the tree?
You come out and bang pans to scare us away, but see—
I don't scare like these other fools.
I preen my oil-blue neck
and patiently watch the seething sun.

When I was small, I could sit in this tree for hours
watching you crutch to the door and raise
your silver bosun's pipe to whistle me home.
I'd won if I could stay in this tree till you'd gone in,
before climbing down and sneaking through the garage.

Suddenly, all I want is to crawl out
of this greasy grackle skin
back through that garage.
But I've perched too high for that.
These branches would crack and I'd fall.

I've grown too old for petty victories;
I could fly over and shit on your car
but you'd only curse all birds and
never know it was me.

I ruffle my feathers against the cold.
I cock my head at the moon.
My talons dig deep into the branch I'm on
and I shiver at the thought of my pride.
It is night, and time to strike.

The Silences

for Mildred Allen

I try to write of silence
and realize the one who really knows it
is my grandmother.

At 94, alone in a California nursing home,
her whole body is silent. She

—once 5'8" now bent
and curved, not unlike a fetus,
osteoporosis—

knows the silence. "Grandmom,
will you come for a ride along the coast?"

"Yes." Hardly a whisper
an exhalation of breath across her tongue,
the only word she has spoken today.

Polio

I imagine it this way:

Driving east from Des Moines
on Highway 6, which will later be I-80
in a convertible roadster, probably a Ford,

the luggage strapped to the side
seems almost to brush the corn,
and the nausea felt just outside Joliet

is blamed on the road
the loss of his land legs
or driving too fast.

Later, in the Chicago hospital
my father reflects that he's come
halfway across the continent.

Now he'll have to give up
the dog he found,
his mechanic's uniform…

Reverence

In 1941, when the medium came down
to Alton, Iowa with the relatives from Montreal,

my father, my grandmother,
and the whole family
was certain she was a hoax.

But even now, after 40 years,
they still speak of her with respect.

"She was good for Aunt Sarah
who lost two sons in the war."

Kelder Jazz

In the cellar of Café de Krieze
they jammed blue notes
that echoed off whitewashed brick arches,
glittered in wine-bottle candle flames,
and mingled with the murmur
of hushed voices, laughter, and tapping feet.

Here I looked into dark Belgian beer,
smelled the cool earth, drank
a draught, and wrote:

I stand in our garage. The smell
of fresh varnish from my father's
crutches welcomes me. I
stick to them as I brush by
in the dark, touching home.

A poem scrawled on paper scraps,
Belgian train tickets, receipts,
addresses of friends who have moved,
jammed in my wallet in *wanorder*,
which in Dutch almost means disarray.

On the Back Burner

for Frances Schultz

The death of a mother must be
packed gently into her silver
tea ball, dowsed in warm water
in her samovar, and set
on the back burner to steep.

There are undertakers to see
in their black suits and forlorn faces,
forms to fill out, and certificates to sign.
The preacher must be seen.
Mother would want it that way.

And after she is safely
buried away, I can gingerly take
a cup from her china cabinet
and slowly sip the bitter tea.

Oasis

Introspection

She has not come here for love,
nor have I.
I've come to write poetry;
she to read.
All that we share
is a desire for coffee
early on a Sunday.

And yet
I find my eyes drifting up
with frequent regularity.
Does the muse reside in her straight brown hair
bundled tightly at the nape of her neck?
Or rest on her glasses stays?
Or dance in her fingers
flipping through the Sunday paper?

Could it be that I'm fooling myself?
Is poetry just another way of picking up chicks?
Is sitting alone at diner tables
all over Chicago looking sensitive
just another version of Rush Street
bare-chested, gold-chained swinging?
Are the words just saying,
"Hey baby!   Hey baby!"
in another language?

She sips at her café mocha.
I fondle my pen.
Hey baby? Hey baby?

In Copenhagen

In Copenhagen, cool rain
on the green bronze face
of the little mermaid. The tourists
huddle inside cafés.
No snapshots can be taken today.

But what would I give to walk
by the harbor with you, to stand
and watch her awhile, to feel
the cool drops on my face and the tip
of my tongue, and to touch your hand.

Or to drink Tuborg Red
from a bottle in a jazz café
with you and get lost in the percussion
of some Latin group that plays
nonstop until long after midnight.

I've done such things with your brother,
long before the night I met you
and got lost in your eyes, one brown,
one blue, and in your voice as we talked
nonstop until long after midnight.

But I'm here in the Hawkeye Diner
drinking coffee from a styrofoam cup,
and the rain that falls outside
is mixed with snow and ice.

Bus Scene

In every Iowa town
the bus passes through
I see a church that says,
"Unauthorized vehicles
will be towed away."

The sounds outside are stifled
by exhaust gray dirt that covers
the snow around the parking lots
where immaculate people go to pray.

In one Iowa town, I see you
climb on the bus, walk
down the aisle, and ask,
"Excuse me, is this seat taken?"

"No," I say. I stare out
at the fields. I try to
remember to breathe.

Where is the fat lady who snores, plasters
me to the window, and subjects me to tales
of her garden? Where are those churches
when I need something to get angry about?

There is only you, smiling,
"Hi, my name is Judy." Only
your elbow grazing my arm.

Objects

She didn't think we were made
for each other, her friend and I.
I asked if she was in love with me.
That was my biggest problem then;
I was far too honest.
I should've asked if she was jealous.

We all spent the night together once,
she in one room of the big old house,
her friend and I in another.
And in the morning, when we'd each
realized we would never make love,
we all parted friends.

Yet somehow, years later,
I ended up with her TV,
some cleaning solution, and a plant.
Just as if we'd gotten a divorce.

Even if you want to remain invisible,
people will still lay objects at your feet.
And whether you think you're a god,
or merely mortal, you still have to find
someplace to put them.

Muskmelon

When one person leaves
       before the other there is a
             silence like a cantaloupe,
      sweet pregnant smell of musk
      hangs on the furniture.

      Skin soft, wet,
slices kisses half-remembered.
      Seeds string beads
      around your body,
stick to my hands
      my hair
      my eyes.

The taste of flesh
      lingers on the tongue
as you stand in the doorway,
         smiling.

Oasis

There are rattlesnakes
    in your kitchen this morning,
        the air is dry
    and the sun glares
    between monolith
        table legs,
    as if the distance between us
        were only
    a five day's walk with no water.

Me, I kick my foot for an
    eon against your chair,
    the bridge of my nose
        whitens,
    my ribs begin to protrude, I can
    feel the marrow draining
        from them, there is
        sand beneath my eye
        sockets and I
    can't stop smiling.
"More

coffee?" you ask, and
in the sound of your voice
I smell a storm brewing.

Song of the Carp

Lying on the bank, my gills fill with mud,
my tongue rots, fragments of lips
hang from my teeth, and my eyes cloud
while staring across the river.

Beautiful words stick in my mouth.
All I can utter are fumes
of methane and rotting leaves.

Maggots crawl through my nose
A cattail sprouts where my brain once was.
Marsh grasses rise from my spine.

So do not spare me the mating flies,
the lice, or the scavenger birds.
Soon I'll be green again, when birches
and aspen reclaim my remains.

The Fragility of Bodies

Time and time again
while I'm driving, someone
will step into the street
and I'll think, if I had passed
a few seconds sooner, I'd know
the fragility of bodies, how flesh
disintegrates on impact, bones
snap right before your eyes.

And time and time again
while walking or riding my bike
a shadow crosses quickly the
corner of my eye and I think,
if that had been a car I'd know
the fragility of my own body.

I don't really know these things.

Mt. Parnassus Chicago

When you have no more beliefs,
what the hell do you write a poem about?

The way snow falls even in the city.
The way pigeons sit facing the wind.
The way the Cubs can be counted on for losing
and music is found up and down Halstead St.

The confines of an el car at five p.m.
The way lines form spontaneously
at Lotto counters everywhere
at the same time every week.

These are all that sustain us now.
The stuff muses are made of—
Well, you have to make do
with what you've got, and really,

what can the muse tell us these days?
She pumps gas at the Seven-Eleven.

City Pastoral

All these cars parked
at the side of the road
signal early morning.

Only the stoplight
is on the street
flashing needlessly red,
green, yellow, red.

The brick wall outside
my window reflects two hours
and forty-nine minutes until
my alarm rings in another day.

There is no reason
to sit in this musty chair.
A car slides by below,
another stranger awake.

As if the phone would ring.
As if my eyes would close.

The Trash Man

No news.
No news no news no news no news.

Hard to find a place to write
Pens don't work
the mind is dead.

> In the morning,
> the trash man—

> All night
> heat
> sweaty sheets, no
> body to stick to.

And if I haven't slept in weeks,
it's not because of you.

In the morning
the trash man comes
and carts away my dreams.

Now That You're Gone

I will come to you as nothing but a shadow
no pretensions of substance, just the sun
dipping below a mountain forming patterns
in the smoke that rises from your ashtray.
And you will hear me as the tapping
of your fingers on the table top.

Let me tell you of a poem that is building
in the eye of a cyclone over Kansas
a nightmare poem of dust and prairie grass.
A poem of grackle wings and dried-up riverbeds.
And let me come as the shadow of a mountain
to blanket you in sleep with my dreams.

These Grackles

These grackles you send me won't speak
they just sit, staring down my sleep.
There must be fifty outside my window,
more on the rooftops and in the catalpa trees.

A flock of thousands follows me;
a great black liquid above my head.

People stare. Never seen such a thing.
Big corn-fed birds. Black demons
from a black mountain of grief.

There is no sound, only wings
flapping like your rivers
rising over floodplains again.

These are my friends, my companions,
my lovers, these grackles
with no need of words.

If one would just land on my shoulder I could
convince him to return with this message:

It's all right.
The game is over.
You can come out now.

But these grackles fly like midnight
crossing the prairies between us to speak
with wings what words will never tell.

Photograph

A woman, standing
with nothing in her hands,
looking into the camera.
No one is behind her.

She wears a dark dress
with bright buttons.
Her collar is open
and the sleeves follow
her arms, the way the
bodice grips her waist.

I can not make out
the lines of her face.
The silver paper has
yellowed. There is a crack
in one corner, where
the sky was folded.

She is holding a smile.
You can see this took
a long time, her eyes
are blurred and her hair
melts around the edges.

She has held her breath
more than a minute,
maybe more than a lifetime.
The photographer has
touched up her eyes
to make her happy.

She has nothing in her hands.
There is no one behind her.
She has held her breath
since the beginning of time.
Surely she can smile
that much longer.

Some Thoughts on Chicago
at Manny's Pancake House

The weight of a sunset
        must be heavier than a skyscraper.
The weight of the lake
        heavier than that.
The weight of a human
        the heaviest of all,
                so when it hails
                the city doesn't burn.

The wind sweeps dead ashes from the streets.
Lightning only scares us when thunder follows too close,
the way that laughter only stings
        when it's too long in coming, and love
                remains at the back of your mind
                like waterfalls storming the medulla.

Under the halo of a street lamp
        two figures hang on one another,
        their bony fingers climbing
                and reclimbing the rungs of spine.
Somewhere in the country
        a woman walks along a river road
                her hands planted at her side,
while on a beach
        three women lift me out of winter
                their conversation clear as the sky.

There is still ice on the water.
The waitress brings more coffee.
An el train thunders through this restaurant,
        a city on wheels.
And outside the cars on Clark Street
        cruise through the raindrops on the window.

There are no answers there,
only questions walking under umbrellas.
So I'm always looking out of Chicago
          at mixmasters leading nowhere
          thumbing rides to daydreams.
And I'm always looking out of Chicago
          till the million voices
          bring me back to this restaurant,
                    this reggae club
                    this poetry show
          this el,
          crashing through the sunset.

Landscapes and Architectures

Fragment

The black dog is silent, no poetry.
The dog cuts out speech. Take me
where this no-speech will go.
Bring me the syntax of whine
and growl, low in the throat.
No words or expressions only this:
a big block of wood. A crack,
a sledge, a wedge would help.

Immobile, this block. Set fire,
set fire; like iron, won't burn.
Too old and gnarled for the saw,
only the ping and crack of metal
on wood can cleave these memories,
not destroy, but sort, stack, and dry
until they rise in a blaze of language,
the flickering tongues of a poem.

It's Merry While Summer Lasts

Mirie it is while sumer ilast
    with fugheles song
Oc nu necheth windes blast
    and weder strong;
Ei, Ei, what this nicht is long!
and ich with wel michel wrong
Soregh and murne and fast.

He'd come out of the north country
        with taconite on his breath
        and rust in his veins.
A son of the Iron Range,
        he flew south on the Yukon Express.
Brother to November,
        he made an early arrival, but somehow
                this Cupid
        wasn't enough for us this year.

We'd already gone off of summer hours.
        Daylight savings time was over.
We thought love could be regulated by an act of Congress,
        turned on or off with that extra hour.
Spring ahead.   Fall back.

So when Cupid came
        with his quiver of iron arrows,
                he missed us.
                We were out.

Sumer is icumen in,
Lhude sing cuccu;
Groweth sed and bloweth med
And springth the wde nu.
Sing cuccu!
Awe bleteth after lomb,
Lhouth after calve cu;
bulluc sterteth, bucke verteth
Murie sing cuccu
cuccu, cuccu,
Wel singes thu, cuccu,
Ne swik thu naver nu.

What you don't understand is
I wasn't looking for love.
I just happened upon it by accident
Really. I only wanted to hear the music,
when I went to those festivals in the park.
The street fairs... were for the street fairs.
Maybe I'd buy some cheap jewelry.
I was in the blues. So why not live them.
I didn't mean to keep seeing your face.
I didn't mean to keep asking you for a light.
It just happened.
So now what?

Foweles in the frith
          the fisses in the flod
  And I mon waxe wod;
Mulch sorwe I walke with
          for best of bon and blod.

You think it's crazy when I mention love
          and fish in one breath.
          I talk about birds—
                    you call me batty.
What you don't understand is
                    what I can't explain.
It came in the wake of a snowstorm.
          It left us stranded.
          The timing
                    was all off. It just
                    happened.

The birds are in the wood.
          The fish are in the flood
  And I'm going nuts;
 I walk with much sorrow
          For the best of bone and blood.

Airport '88, Another Midair Collision

And you—

    A few words escape your mouth.
    What could this mean?
    A new relationship?
    A conversation, nearly.
    Translating thought
    from your internal language
    to hers was never easy.
    The pictures
    blur into words.
    "Hi there."
    "Some heat wave, huh?"

And you are flying back to Chicago.

    This was never meant to happen.
    The script you'd written
    just minutes before
    was for a more coherent character,
    a Carey Grant,
    a suave infidel type.
    Your tie is tight.
    Your hair is falling out.

And you are seated next to a woman

    who is your ex-lover.
    Who is every lover you never abandoned
    every memory of skin
    hair of all colors
    the back of her hands
    the rings
    from many different fingers
    well up in your brain and you—

This was never meant to happen.

A few words escape your mouth.
"I'm in sales."
What could this
mean, you're not
in sales, you
are in an airplane
flying to Chicago.
It is night.
There are no stars.

Who is your ex-lover?

The pictures blur into words.
The film breaks.
The actors leave the set.
There is a fog machine
and a wind machine
blowing in the wings.
This and the altitude
make you dizzy.

A few words escape your mouth.

Your secret language
translated into hers.
"*Ich habe daß nicht gern.*"
"I hate salesmen,"
she is saying.
For once
the blatant tiles of the airport
will come as a welcome relief.

And you are flying back to Chicago.

> The skin
> of an ex-lover
> crawls under yours
> Your hair is falling out.
> There is a fog machine
> and a wind machine,
> or is it the propellers?
> The start of a new relationship?

Some heat wave, huh?

Four Songs for Data Processing

(1)

Some days I just want to
    have a nervous breakdown.
Some days I just want an
    epileptic fit, to lie in the street
    shaking for hours till they take me away
        to a room somewhere: white
        all cool, quiet, and white,
    where someone will feed me,
    where someone will bring in an IV,
    a catheter, some oxygen, an enema,
    where someone will hook up the tubes.
And I can be quiet, think for awhile
    Some days I want to stop living this lie.
    Some days the tubes are already there.
        You just don't see them.
Some days I hide them too well.

(2)

I want a Pentium Processor
for the motherboard in my brain
I want the fast chip
        fastback
        sidekick
        superkey.
I want 640 megabytes of RAM
        expansion memory.
    Sit me down
        with a hand
            on the keyboard.

Let's consider ways
        of reducing downtime.
With appropriate intravenous feeding,
        teeth become unnecessary.
        Perhaps an RS232 serial port
                could be installed.
        With direct neural access (DNA)
                operator error may be
                significantly reduced.

I want a Pentium Processor
for the motherboard in my brain
I want the fast chip
                        fastback
                        sidekick
                        superkey.
        Sit me down
                with a hand
                        on the keyboard.

(3)

Out there in the countryside
        they have a talking Coke machine.
                It knows the time of day.

Out there in the countryside
        they have a bank machine, says,
                "Please wait
                        while your transaction
                                is processing."

Out there in the countryside
        people talk
                and they have a machine
                that dispenses live bait.
        Worms and crawdads for fishing.

(4)

202023
                                    1.69
                    1-8-88
202035
                                    1.69
                    1-8-88
20202020202020202
            6666669   9669   6969
                    888888818881888
202020   (Invoice number)
    1.69   (Shipping amount)
1-8-88   (Shipping date)

                            Any errors?

        Not on the screen.

Breaking Bones

I remember necking once,
out by this airport, where
no planes ever landed.

Thinking of chicken bones and how,
after buying a whole fryer, quartering it,
slicing off each breast, the way the sternum
rises, and the carcass is broken down
bare-handed to be boiled for soup.

Thinking of chicken legs, wings, thighs,
the tenacious cartilage that holds them together,
and how afterwards for days your shoulder blades,
spine, every bone in your body feels strange
during love. Fingers instinctively find the space
where a knife would fit, how the bones
come together or apart.

Thinking of the doctor in the newspaper
clipping my mother sent, how he took
a knife to his wife, scattered her parts
around the basement, pureed her vital organs
because they'd rot too fast, replaced each
brick carefully with the original mortar.

This is, after all, a human body.
These are bones of your bones,
flesh of your flesh; the lips, the tongue,
the curve of a breast fall off in your fingers.

Thinking of the family that kept the father
upstairs for eight years after his death.
Laid on hands, bathed him in oil,
changed his clothes every day.
Eight years they went undiscovered,
until at a Thanksgiving feast, between
the turkey and the mincemeat pie,
the smell of ointments gave him away.

These were real people. These things
really happened in the town
where we were living, down the street,
or in the apartment upstairs.
Afterwards, it's no small victory
to take a shower even by myself.
Making love seems out of the question.

I remember necking once
out by this airport. The sun had set.
A few stars were coming out.
And the crickets sang all night long.

Landscapes and Architectures

1

We feed on the twilight
corner shadows
those five-thirty a.m.
illusions that turn
the hallway into a mansion,
my apartment into a city, the
city into a continent,
the continent into your eyes and other
hollows of your body
as we consume ourselves, the shadows,
and the sun, rising slowly
over our longing.

2

In the early summer of northern Denmark
there is some light in the sky nearly all night long.
There are rolling lunar canyons—dunes
covered with stunted pines and lingon-
berries, crisp as hailstones.
The landscape shivers like a lover
as the mist rolls out
to meet the phosphorescent waves.

3

The names of towns spray painted
on top of buildings,
arrows pointing north,
and water towers
lead the way to the airplane
tree houses I helped build as a kid—
not tree houses, really,
tree cities—maybe twenty platforms
in the old pines out by the burned-out
nursery north of town,
where we lie now
watching across the cornfield
for dust to rise on the gravel road.

4

"In the Midwest
you must be careful,"
a friend once told me.
"The landscape there
can lead a man to drink.
It's not the flatness, per se,
but the way the flatness seems to roll.
It's the space between
windbreaks that draws you in."

5

One winter we took a pile of bricks and broke down the back
wall of an outhouse where we'd discovered a beehive the summer
before. The bees swarmed out, but dropped after a few feet, frozen.
We stood back at a safe distance, waiting for the fresh, cold honey.

6

No.
It is not the windbreaks,
nor the distance between the towns.
It is the creek bed
where the water is sauterne,
the taste of elderberries,
the color of the sun
that shines through my leaded windows
casting rainbows on your
body, from which I drink.

Insomnia

for S. J.

1

Clearing the table
is one solution.
The thermos, tea
pot, kettle, hot
pad, cup, glass,
the empty aluminum-foil wrapper
from a Constant Comment Tea
bag (used, still in the pot).

These and the candle light
—Andrés Segovia—
smells of manicotti and your period.
Wipe them up slowly, gently,
with warm, soapy water.

2

The sounds a new apartment makes:
unfamiliar creakings from the family upstairs
the mice in the basement that
find their way into the walls
the furnace that shakes the strangest things
the light in the bathroom you've
tightened a thousand times already
the sound of your own breathing
and your heartbeat
when you're trying to sleep.

Listen to these things.

3

Make no impression
no indelible mark
that cannot be washed away.

4

You in the ocean
for the first time, swimming.
You under a mulberry
tree, eating; fingers
and feet stained purple.
You in the bedroom;
bread in the oven, rising.

Stars

I sharpen
my shadow
beyond
its one dimension
to carve
from this darkness
the crystal stars
you find
in a handful of topsoil.

Is it the scent
I remember,
or the cleft
of your humid earth?

Along the mauve brooks,
America's landscapes lie.
Fence rows stretch to infinity.

Our love falls,
a steady drizzle,
in a hiding January.

Outside my apartment
a cat yowls in heat or
at being abandoned to the cold.
Inside, I ponder our separation:
These stars are everywhere.

Will the ones I send
already turn to dust
before they reach you?

And will you recognize these tears,
when they dissolve in yours?

In Your Sunset

The surrealism of driving...

The surrealism of driving
for 20 hours is impossible
to get down.
It would take days, maybe,
of driving, stopping to eat,
sleep, and write.

Which is another surrealism altogether.

After 20 hours
there is no sensation.
The sunrise
surprises you.

This was night you were driving through?

And slowly, when you reach your destination,
as you emerge from the cockpit of your car
—not recognizable as a Dodge anymore—
into your lover's arms, your right foot
begins to relax, then your ankle
shin, knee, hip, thigh.

And finally, after days,
when the numbness in your brain
begins to clear, you realize
you will soon do this all again

on your way home.

A Common Occurrence

The severed carcass of a dog
on the highway. Or a possum;
it's hard to tell—
just four feet, an
animal with intestines,
a snout, teeth.

I remember we drove
through the two halves,
Blood smeared across our lane.
You were asleep—
no thud to wake you.
I missed it, all but the softer parts,
which were probably smashed already.

I closed my eyes for a second, too.
This was the fifteenth roadkill I had seen in two days.
After driving twenty hours, they start to multiply.

The hawk
that flew within inches of the car
was real. The other eyes,
later, and the wings,
the deer leaping at me, these
were signals.

Tie-Dye

When we tie-dyed it was not
out of a longing for another decade;
it was simply out of longing.
We live in the present now,
and I'm learning to wear colors
other than blue.

Your mother has inadvertently given us
a new euphemism for sex,
and the shirt we made came out wilder
than I could have possibly imagined.

Tangerine and fuchsia
go well together.
The knots we tied create
unpredictable patterns.

I will wear this shirt with the knowledge you
will undo the buttons, because
sometimes, as you told me,
wanting to make love is enough.

Yet things have gotten so complicated since then.
Soon, you'll move to Tucson and we'll start tying
this whole country up, like the flag
we kept wanting to tie-dye or the fireworks
display we watched on the 4th of July.

Only this time the skyrockets
will be silent, and bearable.
And this time the patterns won't hold
after the knots come undone.

In Your Apartment

There are clouds in your apartment
or the sounds of clouds.
Rather, the air has shape.
Your skin is a violin.

We are making love
to a train whistle
which winds through us.

Inside the wind
a box of chocolates.
Inside the box, roses open.

Inside the house of your ancestors,
you are slowly dripping coffee.

Languor
Only
Varies
Every time

I
see
you.

Love Potion #32

My love lies
on her answering machine
She'll get back to me
if I'll just leave a message
My voice clots
My mind is a blizzard
She is a rock
My paper covers rock
Blizzard covers paper
Scissors cut snow
cut paper
She is a razor
I am cardinal red
My love is an
automatic teller machine
I forgot the secret number

Crackerjack Puzzle

That night
we lay together
on your carpet
with no pressure
like the wire puzzle
from my childhood
that I'm not sure
I know how
to take apart
anymore.

In Your Sunset

Oh that I could put this sunset down!
All Halloween orange over Town
Lake as Tom Waits might say.
But fuchsia, too. We'd just risen
from our first lovemaking
in two months. You had flown
to meet me. I flew, too,
once the hammock broke
and we moved indoors.

Later, by the lake, the clouds
were less like fingers than like the folds
of your vagina, and though the air
was exceptionally cold
for Texas in autumn, I felt warm
within you till the sky grew dark
and it was time to go home.

The Egrets

I would like to show you the great
crookneck birds that roost in the giant
cypress tree whose shade cools the lake.
I think they may be egrets, but who knows?
Plummeting from fantastic heights,
their shit startles me when it hits the water.
A man in a rowboat tells me to watch out
for it. All the fish they eat
really make a stink.

Letter

I sometimes wonder
who got the steamy
love letter you sent
that got lost in the mail.

I hope it was an old woman,
and that she smiled,
folded it up,
and slipped it into an album
with dried wildflowers.

When I'm Old

When I'm old, I imagine I'll spend my time tending flowers: not orchids, but maybe geraniums. All my plants need to be hardy to survive. Perhaps I will have had a wife at some time who has died already or just dried up and blown away over the years. Or maybe there'll have been a succession of lovers, each requiring just a little water and some sunshine to bloom and then be gone. But if I'm lucky I'll have managed to save a few of the bulbs: some iris or maybe tiger lily. And I will have a yard to plant them in, when I'm old.

In a Park

Sometimes I stand the way
I did at twelve, in a park
while two girls walk away.
One will tell me tomorrow
if she will go with me.

Since this is not a very
poetic image, I have
cultivated the green
of the grass, the blue
of the sky, a few red
tulips, so tomorrow
never has to come.

La Luna

The moon in the sky is an old woman
who rests her withered breasts
in the arms of a live oak tree.

But the moon who lies down beside me
is young, her rays, soft like the lips
I remember kiss me all over.

And the moon that you see, my love,
nestled in your palms, is she young or old?
And when she lays her body down
beside yours, both of you
luminescent, what is she?

If she has transformed herself
into a man, I won't mind.

But if she is still a woman,
young or old, I hope she smells of milk
and she caresses your breasts
and kisses you where I would
were I there.

The Coldest January

Habitation

Tonight I put on music,
scan again all the titles
on the bookshelves I constructed,
think of all the manila
envelopes I've mailed,
and roll over to pet my dog.
All these things I do to inhabit
my new apartment in Austin.
The rituals of writing
out the rent check each month,
figuring up the bills—
hardly a beginning.
I bought a table,
put pictures on the walls.
You came to visit once,
and opened the windows to the exhaust
and noise from the expressway.
Somehow I can't take
all of Texas in.
Or the distance between here
and Iowa or the woman I love:
a thousand miles in either direction.

Dream Poem

One evening I lay down thinking,
wouldn't it be nice for once
to dream that one poetic image
which would liberate me to write.
As I slept, I dreamt of a huge black lake,
so big and so black it can't be described.
I was unsure if this was a dream
or if I was really just sleeping,
not dreaming at all, so I felt
around on the banks of my sleep
for a smooth, flat stone to skip
across the surface in the hope
that the ripples, when they collided,
might form that image and tell me
this was the dream I had waited for.
But I couldn't find a stone. The only
things on the shore were the feathers
of a shredded pillow. When I grasped these
one by one and threw them into the lake,
they flew away to form the stars.

Texas Canyon

Who would believe this was Arizona:
six hours out of El Paso, which
it took me all day just to reach,
these boulders belong on another planet.

A sign warns not to paint graffiti,
but the defiant sun spills madder
down the cracks beyond where
halogen lamps create a haven for trucks.

Over by the pay phones the silver keys
and plastic receiver reflect your cool voice.
I'm half an hour out of Tucson, yet I could
stand here talking all night.

When I finally pull back onto the highway
the moon is a thin sliver above cerulean sage
and the sunset, here in the mountains,
inflames the clouds behind me in the east.

Tucson

If I could grasp the sun
that streamed through your kitchen
to light your hair and set
our bodies on fire. Or nap

again on your prickly-pear porch
the way we waited each afternoon
for thunderstorms to roll in over
the mountains and quench our desire.

On Mount Lemmon there are seven
ecozones from the valley to the top,
and though we counted them and compared
each to the proportions of your body,

they are my memories now. Mine alone.
Mesquite is a good wood for burning,
dry, fatty, and fragrant. Sage smoke
drives out unwanted spirits. And saguaro

stand rigidly on the ridge like fetishes.
If I could grasp the sun I'd set
all of Tucson on fire and try
to sleep again in another bed.

The Direction of the Wind

Living in the flight path just six
blocks from the end of the runway,
I can tell the direction of the wind
by where the planes take off and land.

The whine of the engines gradually
becomes nothing more than a natural
lull in the conversation, a noise
to explain when talking on the phone.

Then suddenly, inexplicably this morning
the airlines choose a different path.
I only notice the interminable silence
when without warning a dog begins to howl.

The Siren

No more than a clump of feathers,
after being pelted by last night's hail,
it only takes a little imagination
to resurrect the dead grackle in my yard
into a god, or half-god—even
the sirens were half-human
and only their voices enchanted.

This siren's song must be coupled
with the sound of rain that quenched
more than two month's drought
and finally gave her dried flesh
the chance to decompose.

Once as a mortal, she was too large
for the cats, done in, by pesticides,
car exhaust, or the lack of rain.

Even her fleas abandon her now,
as she is left to softer creatures
and carrion birds who slowly
will carry away her soul.

Cool New Kitchen

Air mail
ceiling fan
bamboo shade
spoon and bowl
listen to the radio
in my new kitchen

the dog won't eat
nothing unusual
and I can feel
the picket fence
in my back where
a lover would

take care of that
old porch light
letters travel nowhere
replies return cooler
than this kitchen
with no A/C

ceiling fan
bamboo shade
bolts and nails
adobe walls
can't keep all
this heat inside

Moon Dancer

Your smile is as sudden
as silence broken
by the sweet
whistle of a bird.

It is twilight
and the moon
two-steps across
bare branches.

You plant magnolias
with your breath,
as the wren of your voice
falls on me like rain.

Persia

In Persia they drink tea
only out of glass glasses;
you can see the color that way.

And yes, it was a woman
who told me this,
but that woman
is not in this poem.

If she were
you might think I loved her,
which may have been true,
but it is not in this poem.

Nor is the golf course
where we walked out
a late night winter's thaw.
Nor the black hairs
curled at her temple.

The moon is in this poem;
it is still a shiver in my sky.
And the tea—
in this poem it is far too dark,
like the taste of curried lentils
or saffron rice.

And I can feel my watch on my wrist.
How often can you feel that? What if
you felt all of your clothes all
at once, all over your delicate body?

You would want to take them off, but
there will be none of that, not in this poem,
no, I could be wearing a parka.
You could see my breath freeze.

That air is in this poem, let me
breathe it for you,
let me taste it as it
melts again my lungs.

For I am in this poem.
And you are in this poem.
Now.

The Coldest January

Even the bread was dry,
hard, white, rough,
like delicious sandpaper when you spread
fresh ricotta on it, so
incredibly bland, with a hint
of what could
or never would have been.

Even the bed
was dry, smoky,
and everyone caught cold.
Neither a deathbed,
nor a cradle
a passionate, passionless
fever full of thistles.

But that denies the taste
of the bread. Or the mozzarella
balls we ate without bread only
olives stabbed on plastic forks.

And it ignores the day at the baths,
the empty opera risers, the mosaics
or the incredible green of the pines,
nearly deciduous.

And the ice
in the bed would melt
like the ice in the fountains.
The coldest January in Rome since the war,
someone said. And Mussolini's
Typewriter would someday be
just another monument
on yet another Japanese
or American camcorder.

Ice, water, ivy, moss
go steadily to work
and even the most diligent
archeologist
is powerless against
the smallest roots.

The letters, the photos
may or may not be in vain.
Time and the temperature
will rise without them.
My heart may thaw
may yet begin to boil,
and your heart, my love, will steam
in your own part of the world.

The Silence of Trees

The deepest silence is to sit
in this empty apartment, sifting
vague memories. The arid landscape
mingles with a few drops of rain
still dripping from the roof,
the sound of the dog scratching,
and the distant rumble of thunder.
This takes me back to the day we
walked on water to sit on a large rock
in the middle of the Pedernales river.

Above on the plains, the Texas sun
scorches cattle and low scrub, but here
the trees bend down to kiss the water,
and you tell me how you and your lover
once found a secluded spot on another river
in another time in Arkansas, how the two
of you stripped down and swam, until
the slam of pickup doors, the wild shouts
of young men, and the crash of boots
through the underbrush made you flee.

If I could, I'd write a poem for the trees,
but I am not in love with a tree; I love
the flutter in your voice, the flash
of your smile like sun on the river,
the intimacy of this moment, as warm
as the rock beneath our backs. I know
doors will slam, voices will reach us,
time's frozen river will shatter back
into motion, and we will run in opposite
directions searching for the same peace.

On Barton Creek

Your body, a pool,
waist deep and
clear enough to swim in.
Or afterwards the sherbet,
ice cold and sweet
like the Texas summer afternoon;
no dust or humidity
in this recollection.

Yet would there be shade
without the sun,
would the creek be cool
without our sweat,
and would I remember
if we had made love?

If I had taken your picture
with the lenses of my hands,
or tasted each of your lovers
melt down my tongue,
would I have tasted the fruit
in the ice or the salt on your skin.

And though I'll never know more
of your love than your shadow
and I'll never know whether this
is a promise or merely the sum
of my own limitations,

on Barton Creek your body
was a pool of clear water, a couple
walked their bicycles through,
and as you joked with the woman
I swam in the shade.

About the Author

Kendall Dunkelberg teaches creative writing and literature at Mississippi University for Women. He grew up in the small town of Osage, Iowa, and has lived in Northfield, Minnesota; Galesburg and Chicago, Illinois; Austin, Texas; Columbus, Mississippi; and Ghent, Belgium. The landscapes and cityscapes of the places he has lived and traveled play a prominent role in his poems.

Dunkelberg earned a BA in English from Knox College and a Ph.D. in Comparative Literature from the University of Texas at Austin. He received a Mellon Fellowship and a Fulbright grant to conduct research in Ghent, Belgium. He has published poems and translations in many literary magazines, including *Slipstream, Osiris, Mudfish, The Literary Review, Dutch Crossing, International Poetry Review, Chiron Review, Quarterly West, Chelsea, Crab Creek Review,* and *Fine Madness*. He served as guest editor of *The Literary Review* for a special issue on recent Dutch and Flemish writing, and Green Integer Press has published *Hercules, Richelieu, and Nostradamus*, a book of his translations of the Belgian poet, Paul Snoek.